The Fall of Saigon

WITHDRAWN

by Mary Englar

Content Adviser: David L. Anderson, Ph.D.,
Professor of History,
California State University, Monterey Bay

Reading Adviser: Rosemary Palmer, Ph.D.,
Department of Literacy, College of Education,
Boise State University

Compass Point Books ✦ Minneapolis, Minnesota

Compass Point Books
151 Good Counsel Drive
P.O. Box 669
Mankato, MN 56002-0669

On the cover: Victorious North Vietnamese troops entered Saigon at the end of the Vietnam War.

Editor: Julie Gassman
Page Production: Ashlee Suker
Photo Researcher: Robert McConnell
Cartographer: XNR Productions, Inc.
Library Consultant: Kathleen Baxter

Art Director: LuAnn Ascheman-Adams
Creative Director: Keith Griffin
Editorial Director: Nick Healy
Managing Editor: Catherine Neitge

Library of Congress Cataloging-in-Publication Data
Englar, Mary.
  The fall of Saigon / by Mary Englar.
     p. cm. — (We the people)
  Includes index.
  ISBN 978-0-7565-3843-9 (library binding)
1. Vietnam War, 1961–1975—Juvenile literature. 2. Vietnam War, 1961–1975—United States—Juvenile literature. I. Title. II. Series.
  DS557.7.E534 2008
  959.704'342—dc22   2008006285

Visit Compass Point Books on the Internet at *www.compasspointbooks.com*
or e-mail your request to *custserv@compasspointbooks.com*

TABLE OF CONTENTS

FINAL EVACUATION!

On April 30, 1975, the roof of the U.S. Embassy in Saigon shook as helicopters set down on the landing pad. One after the other, the pilots guided their copters onto the pad. Just below, embassy staff burned important papers in incinerators, and the smoke and ash spewed into the air. In the distance, the Americans could see the fires burning at the airport from exploding artillery shells.

That spring, the North Vietnamese Army (NVA) had invaded and captured most of South Vietnam. By April, NVA forces had surrounded Saigon, the capital city. Throughout the final battle between North and South Vietnam, American Ambassador Graham Martin hoped to negotiate with North Vietnamese officials to save the government of South Vietnam.

But on April 29, Martin realized that the North Vietnamese wanted total surrender. He ordered all Americans to evacuate Saigon immediately. However, he

North Vietnamese Army tanks rolled down the streets of Saigon as the NVA took control of the city.

had waited so long to give the order that the NVA forces had nearly destroyed the runways at Saigon's airport. Evacuation airplanes could no longer land safely. The final evacuation would have to be by helicopter.

For the next 18 hours, helicopters flew between Saigon and U.S. aircraft carriers offshore. The city was filled with talk about the Americans leaving for good. The

Helicopters carried people to Navy ships in the South China Sea.

South Vietnamese who had worked for the Americans during more than 10 years of war rushed to the airport and the embassy to try to get out of the country. The Americans tried to keep order and evacuated as many people as they could.

By 3:30 A.M. on April 30, several hundred Vietnamese and 150 U.S. Marines remained at the embassy. The helicopter pilots were exhausted. Back in the United States,

ABOUT THE WAR

The Vietnam War was fought from 1959 to 1975. South Vietnam battled the communist Viet Cong of the South and the communists of North Vietnam. (Communists believe in an economic system in which goods and property are owned by the government and shared in common. Communist rulers limit personal freedoms to achieve their goals.)

The Viet Cong and the North Vietnamese wanted to unite the two countries into one communist nation. They were backed by the Soviet Union and China. The United States supported the South Vietnamese with money and troops. The first American combat troops arrived in 1965. By early 1968, there were more than 500,000 U.S. troops fighting in Vietnam.

The fighting grew costly in lives and money. Protests against the war increased. In 1973, a cease-fire agreement was reached, and U.S. troops were withdrawn. Fighting continued, however, until 1975, when the North took control of a united Vietnam.

The war killed more than 58,000 Americans and between 2 million and 4 million Vietnamese. More than 300,000 Americans were wounded during the war, the longest in U.S. history. The effects of the long, bloody war are still felt today.

President Gerald Ford ordered that no more Vietnamese could be evacuated. The last flights would take only the Marines. The Marines quietly spread the word to retreat to the roof for evacuation.

Slowly, the Marines backed up across the court-yard in front of the embassy. The Vietnamese saw that they were being left behind.

President Gerald Ford (1913–2006)

They charged the embassy door. The Marines slammed it shut, barring it behind them. Racing up the stairs, the Marines pulled and locked gates on each floor. Finally, the Marines climbed aboard helicopters on the roof.

The last 11 Marines had to wait nearly two hours for a helicopter. "We were sitting ducks up there," remembered

Marines stood guard to keep South Vietnamese people from climbing over the embassy wall.

Master Sergeant John Valdez. The men discussed what they might do if no one picked them up. But at 7:45 A.M., they spotted a helicopter on the eastern horizon. After they hopped aboard, it headed out to sea. The men saw North

Vietnamese tanks below them, lining the roads into Saigon.

During the final evacuation, 70 helicopters carried more than 1,000 Americans and nearly 6,000 Vietnamese to safety. Despite the largest helicopter evacuation in history, several hundred Vietnamese employees were left behind at the embassy. Ambassador Martin's last-minute evacuation order led to chaos and fear in Saigon.

Vietnamese employees and their families around Saigon panicked as they realized they had been left behind. They did not know what the North Vietnamese would do to them when they took over. But after years of civil war between the North and the South, most did not like their chances.

WINNING THE PEACE

By early 1968, the United States had more than 500,000 soldiers in Vietnam. All young men had to register for the draft at age 18. Often they were drafted into the armed forces and sent to Vietnam. Americans protested the war in the streets of Washington, D.C., and around the country. Many protesters were young adults on college campuses.

Every night, the national news showed bloody battles,

Journalist Dan Rather reported from Vietnam on what was sometimes called the living room war. For the first time, TV viewers watched nightly war reports from their living rooms.

11

President Richard Nixon made a surprise visit to U.S. soldiers in South Vietnam in 1969.

dead soldiers, and Vietnamese civilians forced from their
homes. Americans were growing tired of losing their soldiers
in a war that seemed hopeless and endless. They began to
doubt that the war was worth the cost in dollars and lives.
In November 1968, Richard Nixon won the presidential
election and took office in January 1969. He promised to
"end the war and win the peace."

Nixon soon faced the same problems in Vietnam
that President Lyndon Johnson had faced before him.

North Vietnamese officials believed that the United States would tire of the war and their losses. Nixon did not want to lose the war to the communists, but he could not find a military solution.

In 1969, thousands of antiwar protesters marched in Washington, D.C., and in New York, Boston, and

Antiwar protesters gathered in Washington, D.C., on the day of President Nixon's inauguration.

Detroit. The U.S. Congress passed resolutions demanding that the president withdraw all troops from Vietnam by the end of 1970. President Nixon knew he had to find a way out.

In February 1970, Nixon sent Henry Kissinger, his national security adviser, to meet with North Vietnamese delegates in Paris, France. Le Duc Tho, a founder of the Vietnamese Communist Party, negotiated for the North Vietnamese. Kissinger hoped to secure a cease-fire between the two sides. Tho wanted the Americans to leave South Vietnam.

For more than two years, Kissinger and Tho tried to find an agreement that would end the conflict. Tho knew that Americans were tired of the war, and he pushed for a new government in South Vietnam. Kissinger refused. He hoped to protect the government of South Vietnam, even if the United States withdrew its troops.

Finally, on January 27, 1973, Tho and Kissinger signed the Paris Peace Accords. They agreed to a cease-fire,

Le Duc Tho and Henry Kissinger shook hands in greeting during the Paris Peace Accords.

the withdrawal of all U.S. troops, and an exchange of prisoners of war. North Vietnam had held nearly 600 American prisoners for up to nine years. However, the agreement allowed the North Vietnamese troops to stay in South Vietnam. They had to stop fighting, but they did not have to pull out their troops.

AN UNEASY TRUCE

South Vietnam's President Nguyen Van Thieu initially refused to sign the peace agreement because it did not include a withdrawal of North Vietnamese troops. Nixon told him to sign or risk losing American support in the form of money and weapons. Thieu signed the agreement, but he believed it was a temporary pause in the ongoing war.

At the time of the cease-fire, Thieu's Army of the Republic of Vietnam (ARVN) controlled about 75 percent of the land in South Vietnam. Thieu planned to fight to

President Nguyen Van Thieu (1923–2001)

recapture the land they had lost to the communists. He had no plans to make peace with his enemies, either those in South Vietnam or the government of North Vietnam.

Though both Nixon and Kissinger had promised

At the time of the Paris Peace Accords, South Vietnam still had control of most of its major cities.

President Thieu that the United States would continue military and economic aid, the U.S. Congress realized that most Americans wanted to end all military involvement in Vietnam. In June 1973, Congress voted to block all money used for military support to Vietnam. As the supply of weapons decreased, the South Vietnamese army began to cut back on what it gave to its soldiers. Some ARVN troops lost hope that the United States supported their struggle against communism.

North Vietnamese officials began planning for a final war to unite the two Vietnams. They held territory on the western border of South Vietnam. They built a new road through the jungles and mountains. The road connected North Vietnam with the Mekong Delta in the south. The North Vietnamese also built an oil pipeline to carry fuel and a radio network to communicate with their generals in South Vietnam.

By the fall of 1974, the North Vietnamese began raiding South Vietnam's airports and weapons stockpiles.

Despite being forced to resign from the presidency, Nixon raised his hands in his signature V sign, used to symbolize victory.

ARVN troops fought back, but neither side gained much ground. The small battles drained South Vietnam's supply of ammunition and weapons.

President Nixon had many things on his mind in the summer of 1974. He had been accused of secret criminal government activities. As Congress moved to impeach him, Nixon resigned on August 9, 1974. He tried to save the aid promised to South Vietnam. However, Congress, knowing what the American people wanted, voted for much less money than Nixon had promised.

NORTH VIETNAM ATTACKS

At the beginning of March 1975, South Vietnamese and American officials in Saigon knew that North Vietnam had moved large numbers of troops into South Vietnam. They expected an attack but did not know where the NVA would strike first. North Vietnamese General Van Tien Dung moved his tanks and men into place. Surprise worked in his favor.

Early on the morning of March 10, the people of the small city of Ban Me Thuot woke up to the sound of artillery. No one suspected that the attack would be there, in

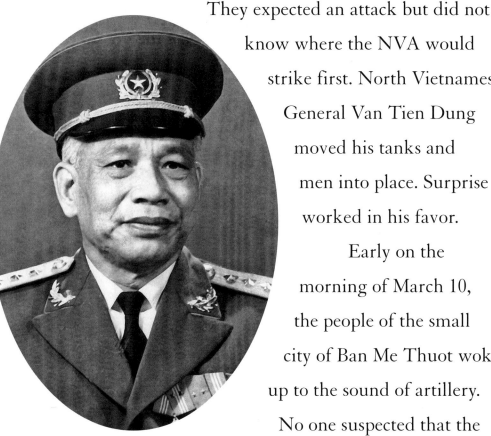

General Van Tien Dung (1917–2002)

the Central Highlands. The battle trapped nine Americans in the city. They huddled in the basement of an American official's house, calling for help by radio.

American officials tried to send in helicopters to get them out, but it was too dangerous. On March 11, NVA soldiers cut the lock on the front gate. They ordered the Americans out of the house and took them prisoner. The youngest prisoner, a 5-year-old girl, clutched her mother's hand and cried. The Americans were held prisoner for eight months.

President Thieu called his military advisers to a meeting in Saigon. He knew that his

Refugees fled the area after Ban Me Thuot fell to North Vietnam.

21

army was stretched thin trying to protect the entire country. In addition to the attacks in the Central Highlands, reports were coming in of other attacks near Danang, the second-largest city in South Vietnam.

Thieu decided to pull his army back from the highlands to protect Saigon and important coastal cities. He did not want to fight for the highlands. Thieu did not ask his American military advisers. He did not even tell them of his plan. On March 14, he told General Pham Van Phu, commander of the central region of South Vietnam, to retreat with his army to the coast. General Phu returned to his post at Pleiku, the main ARVN base in the Central Highlands.

That evening, Phu informed four of his officers that the ARVN forces must withdraw from the highlands. He told them to plan the withdrawal. The next morning, Phu boarded a plane and left Pleiku. He did not tell the Americans or any other officers that he was leaving. By leaving right away, General Phu left his army without a leader.

Phu's officers spread the word that the army was leaving Pleiku. Many of the people in Pleiku were South Vietnamese soldiers and their families. There were some civilians as well. If the army left, no one would be protected from the North Vietnamese Army. Panic set in.

The next evening, more than 100,000 South Vietnamese headed out of the city. It was 150 miles

As villagers fled Pleiku, they were in constant danger of NVA attacks.

23

The refugees overloaded vehicles, making falling off a risk. When people did fall, they were often crushed by the vehicle following behind.

(240 kilometers) to the coast, and many were on foot. The ARVN troops and their families led the convoy. The civilians followed on motorcycles or pushed carts with their belongings. The convoy had to take a dangerous mountain

road to avoid the NVA troops in the area.

NVA General Dung ordered an attack on the convoy. When the convoy stopped at a destroyed bridge in the mountains, communist forces began shelling it. The shells killed as many civilians as soldiers. People fled into the jungle to avoid the shells.

The withdrawal from Pleiku was planned poorly. People carried food and some water, but it took more than a week to reach the coast. Many people died from hunger and thirst. In all, only 60,000 made it to the coast. The rest either died or fled into the jungle to escape.

General Ngo Quang Truong, commander of the ARVN forces in the northern region of South Vietnam, met with President Thieu on March 19. Refugees from north of Danang had clogged the highways. General Truong could not move troops and armor along the main highway. Thieu told him to hold his position at Hue and Danang, no matter what. These cities were the most important ones in the northern part of South Vietnam.

General Ngo Quang Truong's headquarters were in Hue.

But the next day, Thieu told Truong to abandon Hue and to protect Danang at all costs. The NVA forces were moving quickly throughout South Vietnam, and Thieu had decided to protect the south, including Saigon. General Truong ordered his men to abandon Hue and make their way to Danang, but the confusing orders from Thieu made it impossible for Truong to protect either city.

The families of ARVN soldiers lived in Danang where the men were stationed. Wives and children were in danger as the NVA forces approached. Adding to the confusion, Danang filled with refugees, now coming from both the north and the south. After only 10 days of fighting, more than 1 million South Vietnamese were fleeing their homes to escape the NVA attacks.

On March 25, the North Vietnamese began shelling Danang. The airport and harbor filled with people trying to escape. The American consulate officials worked to get thousands of Americans and their South Vietnamese employees on planes or boats. In just three days, the NVA surrounded Danang.

Hundreds of boats picked up people from the waters off Danang. Some were sent by the U.S. Navy to help with the evacuation. Others were fishing boats that could carry only a few people. The refugees in Danang were so frightened, they tried to swim out to the boats. Many people drowned in the sea. By March 29, rescue boats had picked up more than 30,000 refugees. The boats headed south with little water or food for the thousands of frightened refugees.

With the fall of Danang, the NVA troops had

A barge carried Vietnamese refugees from Danang to the SS Pioneer Contender.
The ship then carried the people farther south to Cam Ranh Bay, which was still secure.

gained much of South Vietnam. The North Vietnamese
had not planned to take Saigon in 1975. But the easy vic-
tories and the retreating ARVN troops convinced North
Vietnamese officials to push on. North Vietnam's General
Dung was ordered to take Saigon by the last week of April.
Government officials in Hanoi knew that they had to suc-
ceed before the rainy season slowed their tanks and soldiers.

THE HO CHI MINH CAMPAIGN

In the first week of April 1975, North Vietnam had nearly 300,000 troops in South Vietnam. Another 30,000 waited just north of the border. General Dung planned to take control of the main roads into Saigon. This would cut off Saigon from its military bases outside of the city. The new campaign was named Ho Chi Minh, to honor the former North Vietnamese leader.

On the other side, ARVN forces numbered roughly 90,000. Many ARVN troops had been killed or had abandoned their posts in the preceding weeks. About half of their warplanes and helicopters had been left behind in the retreat to the south. Thieu ordered the remains of the ARVN forces to regroup and stand ready to defend Saigon.

On April 10, about 40,000 NVA troops attacked the city of Xuan Loc, 30 miles (48 km) northeast of Saigon. Despite being far outnumbered, the ARVN fought bravely. They repeatedly pushed the NVA back. The ARVN held the important city until April 21, when they were forced to retreat.

As the NVA forces closed in on Saigon, American Ambassador Martin still believed that the North Vietnamese would agree to a cease-fire. American officials

ARVN soldiers and their families were evacuated from Xuan Loc by helicopter.

offered several proposals to the North Vietnamese. But North Vietnam's leaders knew that they were stronger. They wanted a complete surrender.

Finally, Martin discussed Saigon evacuation plans with President Gerald Ford. Martin knew he could evacuate all the Americans, but there was not enough time to get all the South Vietnamese employees out. The employees would not leave without their families. In April, U.S. Embassy officials evacuated hundreds of Vietnamese on daily flights. More than 50,000 Americans and South Vietnamese left Saigon in March and April 1975.

On April 21, President Thieu resigned and turned the government over to his vice president, Tran Van Huong. Four days later, Thieu and his family left Vietnam and flew to Taiwan. On April 28, Huong turned the government over to General Duong Van Minh. South Vietnamese officials believed General Minh could negotiate with the North Vietnamese.

The people of Saigon could hear artillery explosions

Initial evacuations from Saigon were orderly, with people waiting outside the embassy to board buses to the airport.

from an ARVN base north of the city. As more Americans evacuated, many South Vietnamese worried that they would be trapped in Saigon. Early on the morning of April 29, North Vietnamese pilots bombed the airport. The explosions left craters in the runways, and many planes were on fire.

By 9 A.M., all of Saigon was on the move. Cars, trucks, and motorcycles clogged the streets as people looked for a

way out of the city. Ambassador Martin drove to the
airport to see if evacuation planes could land. The bombing
continued, and Martin realized it was too late. The only
option left was to use helicopters.

Around 11 A.M., Martin agreed to a total evacuation
by helicopter. The evacuation would begin at the airport,

North Vietnamese soldiers ran past damaged airplanes at the bombed-out airport.

Ambassador Graham Martin spoke to reporters after his own evacuation on April 30, 1975.

where people had been waiting for two days. When the airport was cleared, the helicopters then would pick up people at the embassy. Marines chopped down a tree in the embassy parking lot to make room for the large helicopters. Additional small helicopters would take people from the roof.

Embassy employees rushed to destroy documents and equipment they did not want the North Vietnamese to find. They burned secret papers in the rooftop incinerators. They tore maps and photos from the walls and destroyed them. They smashed typewriters, radios, and communication equipment. Other employees formed lines on the stairs to the embassy roof. As each helicopter landed, 20 people ran to get on.

In the courtyard, Marines guarded the embassy gates and lined up on top of the walls. Hundreds of frightened Vietnamese tried to get onto the embassy grounds. But the Marine guards had orders to let only Americans through the gate. They had to push the frightened Vietnamese back

Vietnamese evacuees were helped onto a helicopter perched on top of a building a half-mile (800 meters) from the U.S. Embassy.

from the gates and the walls.

The last day in Saigon frightened both the Americans and the South Vietnamese. Even if they got on a helicopter, they did not know if the North Vietnamese would shoot it down. By the end of the evacuation, no one could take luggage. People left with only the clothes on their backs.

Frank Snepp, an embassy intelligence officer, boarded a helicopter at 9 P.M. He later described his last glimpse of Saigon from the air: "As we veered eastward … the ammunition dump at nearby Long Binh was going up in a succession of miniature atomic explosions, and along the spiderweb of highways leading in from Xuan Loc, I could see literally thousands of trucks and tanks, presumably North Vietnamese."

A UNITED VIETNAM

By the time the last helicopter left the embassy, NVA forces were on the outskirts of Saigon. More than 40,000 NVA troops surrounded the city during the final days. Colonel Bui Tin rode in a tank headed for the Presidential Palace.

When NVA soldiers rolled into Saigon on tanks and trucks, it ended the Vietnam War and reunited the country as a communist nation.

President Duong Van Minh (1916–2001)

His tank crashed through the palace's front gate, and the soldiers jumped out to secure the grounds.

Colonel Tin found President Minh inside the palace. Minh told Tin that he had been waiting for him. He wanted to transfer the South Vietnamese government to the North Vietnamese. Tin answered, "Your power has crumbled. You cannot give up what you do not have." They were interrupted by the sound of gunfire coming from outside the palace. Tin assured Minh that his soldiers were only celebrating. "The war for our country is over," he said.

After Minh surrendered, Saigon was renamed Ho Chi Minh City. More than 200,000 South Vietnamese government workers, police officers, ARVN soldiers, and religious leaders were sent to "re-education camps" to learn about communism. The prisoners were also required to clean toilets, grow rice, and clear away land mines (dangerous work since they often exploded).

The North Vietnamese officials had not expected the

Captured South Vietnamese soldiers were marched down the streets as prisoners.

poverty and unemployment they found in South Vietnam. Years of war had forced many people off their farms and into the cities, resulting in decreased food supplies. Officials sent more than 1.5 million city people to rural communities to increase food production. The new farmers did not have enough housing, food, or medical care.

Americans were shocked by how quickly South Vietnam collapsed. Some cheered the final end to a long, unpopular war. Others argued over who was responsible for the loss of South Vietnam to the communists. Many military leaders accused the president and Congress of not putting enough men and money into the war at the beginning. Other Americans believed the South Vietnamese did not have the will to win.

The Vietnam War divided the American people as no other modern conflict had done. It had cost the United States billions of dollars and more than 58,000 American lives. Many Americans lost confidence in their armed forces, their political leaders, and America's reputation in

Today new apartment buildings are sprouting up in Vietnamese cities. The country is one of the fastest growing nations in the world.

the world. More than 30 years later, America has rebuilt its military strength, and Americans have confidence in their troops. Yet, when the president orders troops into battle, many Americans are reminded of the sharp disagreements that divided the nation during the Vietnam War.

GLOSSARY

artillery—large weapons, such as cannons or missile launchers, that require several soldiers to load, aim, and fire

cease-fire—to end a battle without either side being declared the winner

civilians—people who are not part of a military force

convoy—group of vehicles traveling together, usually accompanied by armed forces

draft—system that chooses people who are required by law to serve in the military

embassy—office for a country's representatives in another country

evacuate—to leave a dangerous place and go someplace safer

impeach—to charge an elected official with a serious crime; it can result in removal from office

negotiate—bargain for an agreement between two countries, such as an end to a war

resolutions—formal opinions voiced by a legislature or committee

DID YOU KNOW?

- Henry Kissinger and Le Duc Tho were awarded the Nobel Peace Prize in 1973 for their peace agreement to end the fighting in Vietnam. Tho refused the prize, saying his country was not yet at peace.

- In April 1975, President Gerald Ford authorized $2 million to bring Vietnamese orphans to America. The first flight crashed shortly after takeoff, killing almost half of the orphans and staff. In all, Operation Babylift brought more than 2,700 orphans to new homes in the United States. Ford met the first flight to land in the United States.

- About 50,000 mixed-race children were born to Vietnamese women and American soldiers during the war. The Vietnamese people rejected these Amerasian children. They could not go to school, and many had to beg for food. By 1990, the children's fathers or foster families had brought most of them to the United States.

- After Saigon fell in 1975, more than 1 million Vietnamese tried to escape from Vietnam. Most left on small fishing boats. If they were lucky, a ship picked them up and brought them to refugee camps in Asia. Many were not picked up and died from thirst, starvation, or drowning.

IMPORTANT DATES

Timeline

1965	In March, first U.S. combat troops arrive in Vietnam
1973	On January 27, Paris Peace Accords end America's military role in Vietnam; in March, last U.S. combat troops leave Vietnam
1974	On August 9, President Nixon resigns
1975	On March 10, North Vietnam attacks the Central Highlands in South Vietnam; on March 30, Danang falls to the North Vietnamese; on April 21, President Thieu resigns and leaves for Taiwan four days later; on April 30, the last U.S. Embassy and military officials evacuate Saigon, and North Vietnam accepts surrender of South Vietnam

IMPORTANT PEOPLE

VAN TIEN DUNG (1917–2002)

North Vietnamese general who was appointed commander in chief of the NVA forces in January 1975; Dung led the successful 1975 attack on South Vietnam's Central Highlands; after the war, he served as the defense minister of Vietnam from 1980 to 1987

HENRY KISSINGER (1923–)

Born in Germany, Kissinger came to the United States in 1938 and became a U. S. citizen in 1943; served as President Nixon's national security adviser from 1969 to 1973, then as secretary of state from 1973 to 1977; he negotiated the 1973 Paris Peace Accords with North Vietnam

NGUYEN VAN THIEU (1923–2001)

Served as president of South Vietnam from 1967 to 1975; he joined the Vietnamese army in the 1940s and trained in France and the United States; he distrusted the American will to protect South Vietnam and repeatedly refused to negotiate with North Vietnam

LE DUC THO (1910–1990)

North Vietnamese official in charge of the Viet Cong communists in South Vietnam; he was a founder of the Vietnamese Communist Party; he negotiated the 1973 Paris Peace Accords with the United States but refused the Nobel Peace Prize

WANT TO KNOW MORE?

More Books to Read

Burgan, Michael. *The Vietnam War*. New York: World Almanac
 Library, 2006.

Canwell, Diane, and Jon Sutherland. *American Women in the Vietnam War*.
 New York: World Almanac Library, 2005.

Caputo, Philip. *10,000 Days of Thunder: A History of the Vietnam War*.
 New York: Atheneum, 2005.

DK Publishing. *Vietnam War: DK Eyewitness Books*. New York:
 DK Publishing, 2005.

Warren, Andrea. *Escape From Saigon: How a Vietnam War Orphan Became an
 American Boy*. New York: Farrar, Strauss, and Giroux, 2004.

On the Web

For more information on this topic, use FactHound.

1. Go to *www.facthound.com*

2. Type in this book ID: 0756538432

3. Click on the *Fetch It* button.

FactHound will find the best Web sites for you.

On the Road

National Vietnam Veterans Art Museum
1801 S. Indiana Ave.
Chicago, IL 60616
312/326-0270
Exhibit of more than 1,500 works of art done by more than 100 artists who have expressed their thoughts and experiences of the Vietnam War

Vietnam Veterans Memorial
National Mall
Washington, DC
202/426-6841
National monument that honors troops killed or missing in Vietnam; Vietnam Women's Memorial is nearby

Look for more We the People books about this era:

The 19th Amendment

The Berlin Airlift

The Civil Rights Act of 1964

The Draft Lottery

The Dust Bowl

Ellis Island

GI Joe in World War II

The Great Depression

The Holocaust Museum

The Kent State Shootings

The Korean War

The My Lai Massacre

Navajo Code Talkers

The Negro Leagues

Pearl Harbor

The Persian Gulf War

The San Francisco Earthquake of 1906

Selma's Bloody Sunday

September 11

The Sinking of the USS Indianapolis

The Statue of Liberty

The Tet Offensive

The Titanic

The Tuskegee Airmen

Vietnam Veterans Memorial

Vietnam War POWs

A complete list of We the People titles is available on our Web site:
www.compasspointbooks.com

INDEX

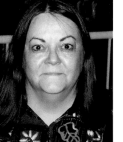

About the Author

Mary Englar is a freelance writer and a teacher of English and creative writing.
She has a master of fine arts degree in writing from Minnesota State University,
Mankato, and has written more than 30 nonfiction books for children. She lives
in Minnesota, where she continues to read and write about the many different
cultures of our world.